The Wit and ^Anti-Wisdom of George W. Bush

A Hysterical Historical Timeline

SOURCEBOOKS HYSTERIA™
AN IMPRINT OF SOURCEBOOKS, INC.®
NAPERVILLE, ILLINOIS

Published by Sourcebooks, Inc.

P.O. Box 4410, Naperville, Illinois 60567-4410

(630) 961-3900

Fax: (630) 961-2168

www.sourcebooks.com

ISBN-13: 978-1-4022-0943-7

ISBN-10: 1-4022-0943-6

Printed and bound in United States of America

LB 10 9 8 7 6 5 4 3 2 1

On the
Campaign Trail

"The important question is, how many hands have I shaked?"

—*New York Times*

Oct. 23, 1999

"Rarely is the question asked: Is our children learning?"

—South Carolina campaign stop

Jan. 11, 2000

"I know how hard it is for you to put food on your family."

—Nashua, New Hampshire

"Will the highways on the Internet become more few?"

—Concord, New Hampshire

Jan. 27,
2000

Jan. 29,
2000

"The most important job is not to be governor, or first lady in my case."

—San Antonio Express-News

Jan. 30, 2000

"We ought to make the pie higher."

—South Carolina debate

Feb. 15,
2000

> ## "I understand small business growth. I was one."
> —*New York Daily News*

> ## "It is not Reaganesque to support a tax plan that is Clinton in nature."
> —Los Angeles, California

Feb. 19,
2000

Feb. 23,
2000

> "I thought how proud I am to be standing up beside my dad. Never did it occur to me that he would become the gist for cartoonists."
>
> —*Newsweek*

Feb. 28,
2000

"Reading is the basics for all learning."

—Reston, Virginia

Mar. 28,
2000

"We want our teachers to be trained so they can meet the obligations, their obligations as teachers. We want them to know how to teach the science of reading. In order to make sure there's not this kind of federal—federal cufflink."

—Milwaukee, Wisconsin

Mar. 30, 2000

"I think anybody who doesn't think I'm smart enough to handle the job is underestimating."

—*U.S. News & World Report*

Apr. 3,
2000

"I was raised in the West. The west of Texas. It's pretty close to California. In more ways than Washington, D.C., is close to California."

Los Angeles Times

Apr. 8, 2000

"I hope we get to the bottom of the answer. It's what I'm interested to know."

—Associated Press

Apr. 26, 2000

"The fact that he relies on facts— says things that are not factual—are going to undermine his campaign."

—*New York Times*

May 4, 2000

"It's clearly a budget. It's got a lot of numbers in it."

—Reuters

May 5,
2000

"Actually, I—this may sound a little West Texan to you, but I like it. When I'm talking about—when I'm talking about myself, and when he's talking about myself, all of us are talking about me."

—*Hardball*

May 31,
2000

"There's not going to be enough people in the [Social Security] system to take advantage of people like me."

—Wilton, Connecticut

June 9,
2000

"This case has had full analyzation and has been looked at a lot. I understand the emotionality of death penalty cases."

—*Seattle Post-Intelligencer*

June 23,
2000

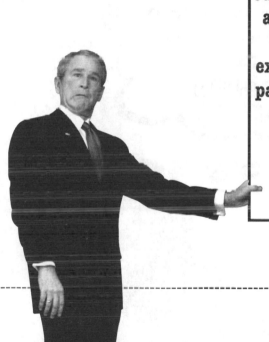

"Unfairly but truthfully, our party has been tagged as being against things. Anti-immigrant, for example. And we're not a party of anti-immigrants. Quite the opposite. We're a party that welcomes people."

—Cleveland, Ohio

July 1, 2000

"I want you to know that farmers are not going to be secondary thoughts to a Bush administration. They will be in the forethought of our thinking."

—Salinas, California

Aug. 10, 2000

"I have a different vision of leadership. A leadership is someone who brings people together."

—Barlett, Tennessee

Aug. 18, 2000

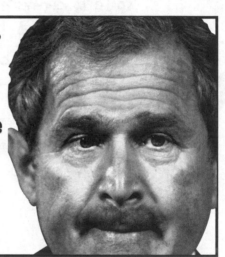

"I don't know whether I'm going to win or not. I think I am. I do know I'm ready for the job. And, if not, that's just the way it goes."

—Des Moines, Iowa

Aug. 21, 2000

"Well, I think if you say you're going to do something and don't do it, that's trustworthiness."

—CNN online chat

Aug. 30, 2000

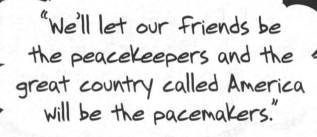

> **"This is what I'm good at.
> I like meeting people, my
> fellow citizens, I like
> interfacing with them."**
>
> —Near Pittsburgh, Pennsylvania

Sept. 8,
2000

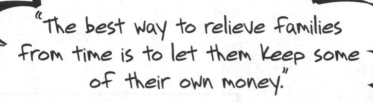

"The best way to relieve families from time is to let them keep some of their own money."

—Westminster, California

Sept. 13, 2000

> ## "A tax cut is really one of the anecdotes to coming out of an economic illness."
>
> —*The Edge with Paula Zahn*

Sept. 18,
2000

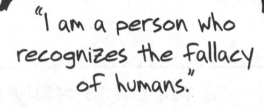

"I am a person who recognizes the fallacy of humans."

— *The Oprah Winfrey Show*

Sept. 19, 2000

> ## "It is clear our nation is reliant upon big foreign oil. More and more of our imports come from overseas."
>
> —Beaverton, Oregon

Sept. 25,
2000

"I mean, there needs to be a wholesale effort against racial profiling, which is illiterate children."

—during the second presidential debate

Oct. 11, 2000

"Families is where our nation finds hope, where wings take dream."

—LaCrosse, Wisconsin

Oct. 18,
2000

"I don't want nations feeling like that they can bully ourselves and our allies. I want to have a ballistic defense system so that we can make the world more peaceful, and at the same time I want to reduce our own nuclear capacities to the level commiserate with keeping the peace."

—Des Moines, Iowa

Oct. 23, 2000

> **"It's important for us to explain to our nation that life is important. It's not only life of babies, but it's life of children living in, you know, the dark dungeons of the Internet."**
>
> —Arlington Heights, Illinois

Oct. 24,
2000

"They want the federal government controlling Social Security like it's some kind of federal program."

—St. Charles, Missouri

Nov. 2, 2000

"They misunderestimated me."

Bentonville, Arkansas

Nov. 6,
2000

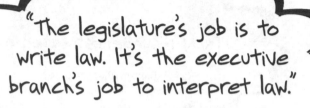

"The legislature's job is to write law. It's the executive branch's job to interpret law."

—Austin, Texas

Nov. 22, 2000

"As far as the legal hassling and wrangling and posturing in Florida, I would suggest you talk to our team in Florida led by Jim Baker."

—Crawford, Texas

Nov. 30, 2000

"The great thing about America is everybody should vote."

—Austin, Texas

Dec. 8,
2000

"If this were a dictatorship, it'd be a heck of a lot easier, just so long as I'm the dictator."

—Washington, D.C.

Dec. 18,
2000

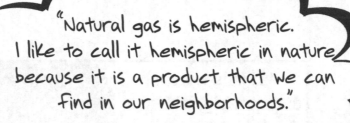

"Natural gas is hemispheric. I like to call it hemispheric in nature because it is a product that we can find in our neighborhoods."

—Austin, Texas

Dec. 20, 2000

> ## "I'm going to work with every Cabinet member to set a series of goals for each Cabinet."
>
> —Austin, Texas

Jan. 2,
2001

"The California crunch really
is the result of not enough power-
generating plants and then not enough
power to power the power of
generating plants."

—*New York Times*

Jan. 14,
2001

"I want everybody to hear loud and clear that I'm going to be the president of everybody."

—Washington, D.C.

Jan. 18,
2001

In the House

> "My pro-life position is I believe there's life. It's not necessarily based in religion. I think there's a life there, therefore the notion of life, liberty, and the pursuit of happiness."
>
> —*San Francisco Chronicle*

Jan. 23,
2001

"I am mindful not only of preserving executive powers for myself, but for predecessors as well."

—Washington, D.C.

Jan. 29, 2001

> ## "It's about past seven in the evening here so we're actually in different time lines."
>
> —*New York Times*

Jan. 30,
2001

"One reason I like to highlight reading is—
reading is the beginnings of the ability to be a
good student. And if you can't read, it's going
to be hard to realize dreams; it's going to
be hard to go to college. So when your teachers
say, read—you ought to listen to her."

—Nalle Elementary School, Washington, D.C.

Feb. 9,
2001

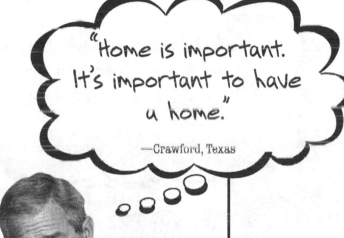

"Home is important.
It's important to have
a home."

—Crawford, Texas

Feb. 18,
2001

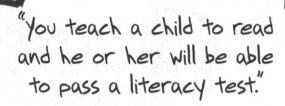

"You teach a child to read and he or her will be able to pass a literacy test."

—Townsend Elementary School,
Townsend, Tennessee

Feb. 21, 2001

> ## "I have said that the sanction regime is like Swiss cheese—that meant that they weren't very effective."
>
> —White House press conference

Feb. 22,
2001

"My plan reduces the national debt, and fast. So fast…that economists worry that we're going to run out of debt to retire."

—National radio address

Feb. 24, 2001

"My pan plays down
an unprecedented amount of
our national debt."

—addressing Congress

Feb. 27,
2001

"It's good to see so many friends here in the Rose Garden. This is our first event in this beautiful spot, and it's appropriate we talk about policy that will affect people's lives in a positive way in such a beautiful, beautiful part of our national—really, our national park system, my guess is you would want to call it."

—in the Rose Garden

Feb. 28,
2001

> **"Ann and I will carry out this equivocal message to the world: Markets must be open."**
>
> —swearing in Ann Veneman as the
> Secretary of Agriculture

Mar. 2,
2001

"I suspect that had my dad not been president, he'd be asking the same questions: How'd your meeting go with so-and-so?...How did you feel when you stood up in front of the people for the State of the Union Address—state of the budget address, whatever you call it."

—*Washington Post*

Mar. 9, 2001

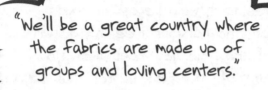

"We'll be a great country where the fabrics are made up of groups and loving centers."

—Kalamazoo, Michigan

Mar. 27, 2001

"I've coined new words, like 'misunderstanding' and 'Hispanically.'"

—Radio & Television Correspondents' Dinner

Mar. 29,
2001

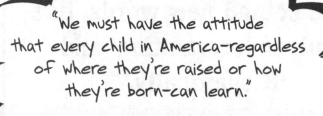

"We must have the attitude that every child in America—regardless of where they're raised or how they're born—can learn."

—New Britain, Connecticut

Apr. 18, 2001

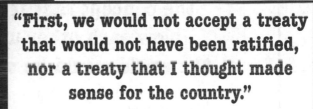

"First, we would not accept a treaty that would not have been ratified, nor a treaty that I thought made sense for the country."

—*Washington Post*

Apr. 24, 2001

"But I also made it clear to him
[Russian President Vladimir Putin]
that it's important to think beyond
the old days of when we had
the concept that if we
blew each other up,
the world would be safe."

—the Rose Garden

May 1,
2001

"There's no question that the minute I got elected, the storm clouds on the horizon were getting nearly directly overhead."

—Washington, D.C.

May 11, 2001

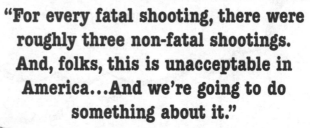

"For every fatal shooting, there were roughly three non-fatal shootings. And, folks, this is unacceptable in America...And we're going to do something about it."

—Philadelphia, Pennsylvania

May 14, 2001

"If a person doesn't have the capacity that we all want that person to have, I suspect hope is in the far distant future, if at all."

—Washington, D.C., Hispanic
Scholarship Fund briefing

May 22,
2001

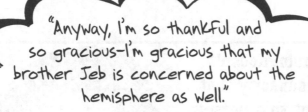

"Anyway, I'm so thankful and so gracious–I'm gracious that my brother Jeb is concerned about the hemisphere as well."

—Miami, Florida

June 4, 2001

> **"Russia is no longer our enemy and therefore we shouldn't be locked into a Cold War mentality that says we keep the peace by blowing each other up. In my attitude, that's old, that's tired, that's stale."**
>
> —Des Moines, Iowa

June 8,
2001

"I haven't had a chance to talk, but I'm confident we'll get a bill that I can live with if we don't... Can't living with the bill means it won't become law."

—Brussels, Belgium, regarding the McCain-Kennedy patients' bill of rights

June 13, 2001

"It's amazing I won. I was running against peace, prosperity, and incumbency."

—during a meeting with the Swedish Prime Minister Goran Persson

June 14, 2001

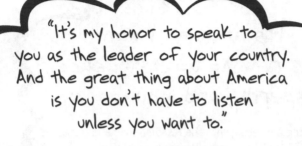

"It's my honor to speak to you as the leader of your country. And the great thing about America is you don't have to listen unless you want to."

—Ellis Island, New York

July 10, 2001

"I know what I believe. I will continue to articulate what I believe and what I believe—I believe what I believe is right."

—Rome, Italy

July 22, 2001

"Brie and cheese."

—Waco, Texas, discussing what he thinks journalists eat

Aug. 23, 2001

> "I'm confident we can work with Congress to come up with an economic stimulus package, if need be, that will send a clear signal to the risk takers and capital formators of our country, that the government's going to act, too."
>
> —Washington, D.C.

Sept. 17,
2001

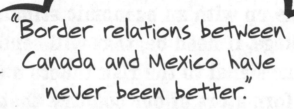

"Border relations between Canada and Mexico have never been better."

—press conference with the Prime Minister of Canada, Jean Chrétien

Sept. 24, 2001

"The folks who conducted to act on our country
on September 11th made a big mistake.
They underestimated America. They underestimated
our resolve, our determination, our love for freedom.
They misunderestimated the fact that we love a
neighbor in need. They misunderestimated
the compassion of our country. I think they
misunderestimated the will and determination
of the Commander-in-Chief, too."

—Langley, Virginia

Sept. 26,
2001

"We are fully committed to working with both sides to bring the level of terror down to an acceptable level for both."

—Washington, D.C.

Oct. 2, 2001

"I am here to make an announcement that this Thursday, ticket counters and airplanes will fly out of Ronald Reagan Airport."

—Washington, D.C.

Oct. 2, 2001

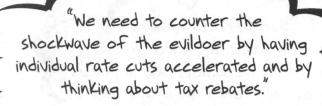

"We need to counter the shockwave of the evildoer by having individual rate cuts accelerated and by thinking about tax rebates."

—Washington, D.C.

Oct. 4, 2001

> ## "The United States and Russia are in the midst of transformationed relationship that will yield peace and progress."
>
> —Washington, D.C.

Nov. 13,
2001

"I couldn't imagine somebody like Osama bin Laden understanding the joy of Hanukkah."

—at the annual White House lighting of the menorah

Dec. 10, 2001

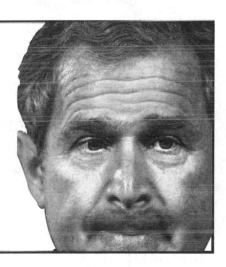

"I want to thank you for taking time out of your day to come and witness my hanging."

—at the dedication of his gubernatorial portrait in Austin, Texas

Jan. 4, 2002

> ## "I've been to war. I've raised twins. If I had a choice, I'd rather go to war."
>
> —Charleston, West Virginia

Jan. 27,
2002

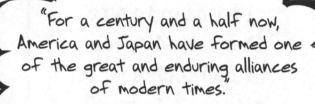

"For a century and a half now, America and Japan have formed one of the great and enduring alliances of modern times."

—Tokyo, Japan

Feb. 18, 2002

"They didn't think we were a nation that could conceivably sacrifice for something greater than our self; that we were soft, that we were so self-absorbed and so materialistic that we wouldn't defend anything we believed in. My, were they wrong. They missed—they just were reading the wrong magazine or watching the wrong Springer show."

—Washington, D.C.

Mar. 12,
2002

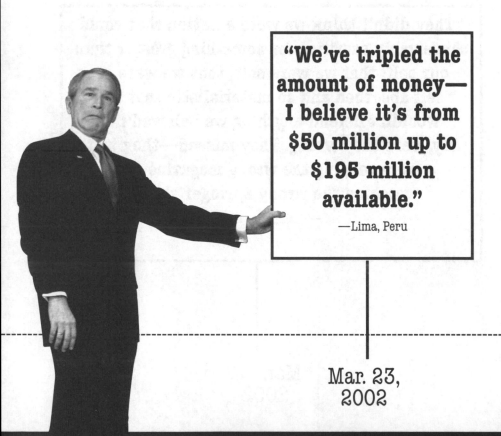

"We've tripled the amount of money— I believe it's from $50 million up to $195 million available."

—Lima, Peru

Mar. 23, 2002

"Sometimes when I sleep at night I think of [Dr. Seuss's] Hop on Pop."

—Pennsylvania State University

Apr. 2, 2002

"And so, in my State of the—my State of the Union—or state—my speech to the nation, whatever you want to call it, speech to the nation —I asked Americans to give 4,000 years— 4,000 hours over the next—the rest of your life —of service to America. That's what I asked— 4,000 hours."

—Bridgeport, Connecticut

Apr. 9,
2002

"I want to thank the dozens of welfare-to-work stories, the actual examples of people who made the firm and solemn commitment to work hard to embetter themselves."

—Washington, D.C.

Apr. 18, 2002

"This foreign policy stuff is a little frustrating."

—*New York Daily News*

Apr. 23, 2002

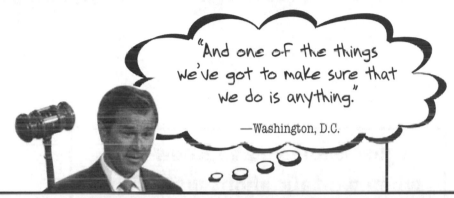

"And one of the things we've got to make sure that we do is anything."

—Washington, D.C.

"The public education system in America is one of the most important foundations of our democracy. After all, it is where children from all over America learn to be responsible citizens, and learn to have the skills necessary to take advantage of our fantastic opportunistic society."

—Santa Clara, California

May 1, 2002

"I just want you to know that, when we talk about war, we're really talking about peace."

—Department of Housing and
Urban Development, Washington, D.C.

June 18,
2002

"There was no malfeance involved. This was an honest disagreement about account procedures...There was no malfeance, no attempt to hide anything."

—White House press conference

July 8, 2002

"The trial lawyers are very politically powerful...but here in Texas, we took them on and got some good medical—
medical malpractice."

—Waco, Texas

Aug. 13,
2002

"I'm a patient man. And when I say I'm a patient man, I mean I'm a patient man."

—Crawford, Texas

Aug. 21, 2002

"See, we love—we love freedom.
That's what they didn't understand.
They hate things; we love things.
They act out of hatred; we don't seek
revenge, we seek justice out of love."

—Oklahoma City, Oklahoma

Aug. 29,
2002

"If you don't have any ambitions, the minimum-wage job isn't going to get you to where you want to get, for example. In other words, what is your ambitions? And oh, by the way, if that is your ambition, here's what it's going to take to achieve it."

—Little Rock, Arkansas

Aug. 29, 2002

"There's no doubt in my mind that we should allow the world's worst leaders to hold America hostage, to threaten our peace, to threaten our friends and allies with the world's worst weapons."

—South Bend, Indiana

Sept. 5, 2002

"There's an old saying in Tennessee—
I know it's in Texas, probably in
Tennessee—that says,
fool me once, shame on—shame on you.
Fool me—you can't get fooled again."

—Nashville, Tennessee

Sept. 17,
2002

"We need an energy bill that encourages consumption."

—Trenton, New Jersey

Sept. 23,
2002

"I need to be able to move the right people to the right place at the right time to protect you, and I'm not going to accept a lousy bill out of the United Nations Senate."

—South Bend, Indiana

Oct. 31, 2002

"I had a cordial meeting at the meeting last night. We greeted each other cordially."

—after meeting with German Chancellor Gerhard Schroeder

Nov. 21, 2002

"Sometimes, Washington is one of these towns where the person–people who think they've got the sharp elbow is the most effective person."

—New Orleans, Louisiana

Dec. 3, 2002

"In other words, I don't think people ought to be compelled to make the decision which they think is best for their family."

—Washington, D.C., regarding smallpox vaccinations

Dec. 11,
2002

"The war on terror involves Saddam Hussein because of the nature of Saddam Hussein, the history of Saddam Hussein, and his willingness to terrorize himself."

—Grand Rapids, Michigan

Jan. 29, 2003

"You're free. And freedom is beautiful.
And, you know, it will take time
to restore chaos and order—order
out of chaos. But we will."

—Washington, D.C.

Apr. 13,
2003

"I don't bring God into my life to-to, you know, kind of be a political person."

—aboard Air Force One

Apr. 24, 2003

"First, let me make it very clear: poor people aren't necessarily killers. Just because you happen to be not rich doesn't mean you're willing to kill."

—Washington, D.C.

May 19, 2003

"I'm the master of low expectations...
I'm also not very analytical.
You know I don't spend a lot of time
thinking about myself, about
why I do things."

—aboard Air Force One

June 4,
2003

"You've also got to measure in order to begin to effect change that's just more—when there's more than talk, there's just actual—a paradigm shift."

—Washington. D.C.

July 1, 2003

"It's very interesting when you think about it, the slaves who left here to go to America, because of their steadfast and their religion and their belief in freedom, helped change America."

—Dakar, Senegal

July 8,
2003

"Our country puts $1 billion a year up to help feed the hungry. And we're by far the most generous nation in the world when it comes to that, and I'm proud to report that. This isn't a contest of who's the most generous. I'm just telling you as an aside. We're generous. We shouldn't be bragging about it. But we are. We're very generous."

—Washington, D.C.

July 16,
2003

> **"And the other lesson is that there are people who can't stand what America stands for, and desire to conflict great harm on the American people."**
>
> —Pittsburgh, Pennsylvania

July 28,
2003

"We had a good Cabinet meeting, talked about a lot of issues. Secretary of State and Defense brought us up to date about our desires to spread freedom and peace around the world."

—Washington, D.C.

Aug. 1,
2003

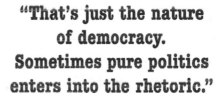

"That's just the nature of democracy. Sometimes pure politics enters into the rhetoric."

—Crawford, Texas

Aug. 8, 2003

"As Luce reminded me, he said, without data, without facts, without information, the discussions about public education mean that a person is just another opinion."

—Jacksonville, Florida

Sept. 9, 2003

"We had a chance to visit with Teresa Nelson who's a parent, and a mom or a dad."

—Jacksonville, Florida

Sept. 9, 2003

"I glance at the headlines just to kind of get a flavor for what's moving. I rarely read the stories, and get briefed by people who are...probably read the news themselves."

—interview with *Fox News's* Brit Hume

Sept. 21, 2003

"See, free nations are peaceful nations. Free nations don't attack each other. Free nations don't develop weapons of mass destruction."

—Milwaukee, Wisconsin

Oct. 3, 2003

"Whether they be Christian, Jew, or Muslim, or Hindu, people have heard the universal call to love a neighbor just like they'd like to be called themselves."

—Washington, D.C.

Oct. 8,
2003

"As you know, these are open forums, you're able to come and listen to what I have to say."

—Washington, D.C.

Oct. 28, 2003

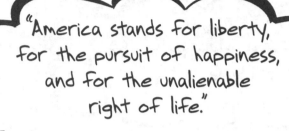

"America stands for liberty, for the pursuit of happiness, and for the unalienable right of life."

—Washington, D.C.

Nov. 5, 2003

"This very week in 1989, there were protests in East Berlin and in Leipzig. By the end of that year, every communist dictatorship in Central America had collapsed."

—Washington, D.C.

Nov. 6,
2003

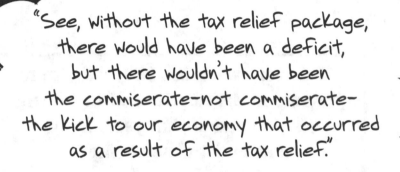

"See, without the tax relief package, there would have been a deficit, but there wouldn't have been the commiserate—not commiserate—the kick to our economy that occurred as a result of the tax relief."

—Washington, D.C.

Dec. 15, 2003

> **"So thank you for reminding me about the importance of being a good mom and a great volunteer as well."**
>
> —St. Louis, Missouri

Jan. 5,
2004

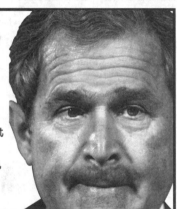

"I was a prisoner, too, but for bad reasons."

—Monterrey, Mexico, to President Nestor Kirchner of Argentina upon learning that he was once a prisoner of the old regime

Jan. 13, 2004

"I want to thank
the astronauts who are with us,
the courageous spacial entrepreneurs
who set such a wonderful example
for the young of our country."
—NASA Headquarters, Washington, D.C.

Jan. 14,
2004

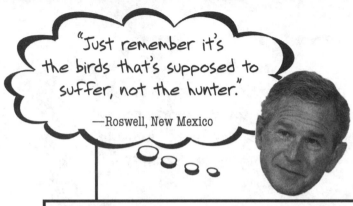

"Just remember it's the birds that's supposed to suffer, not the hunter."

—Roswell, New Mexico

"Then you wake up at the high school level and find out that the illiteracy level of our children are appalling."

—Washington, D.C.

Jan. 22, 2004

Jan. 23, 2004

"My views are one that speaks to freedom...
More Muslims have died at the hands of killers
than—I say more Muslims—a lot of Muslims have
died—I don't know the exact count—at Istanbul.
Look at these different places around the world
where there's been tremendous death and
destruction because killers kill.

—Washington, D.C.

Jan. 29,
2004

"There is no such thing necessarily in a dictatorial regime of iron-clad absolutely solid evidence. The evidence I had was the best possible evidence that he had a weapon."

—*Meet the Press*

Feb. 8,
2004

"Joe, I don't do nuance."

—*Time Magazine*,
to Senator Joseph Biden

"Recession means that people's incomes,
at the employer level, are going down,
basically, relative to costs, people
are getting laid off."

—Washington, D.C.

Feb. 15,
2004

Feb. 19,
2004

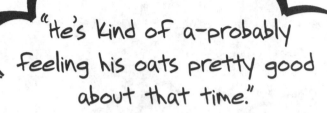

"He's kind of a-probably feeling his oats pretty good about that time."

—at the Faith-Based and Community Initiatives Conference, Los Angeles, California, describing when Rabbi Mark Borovitz met his wife, Harriet

Mar. 3, 2004

"The march to war hurt the economy.
Laura reminded me a while ago that
remember what was on the TV screens—
she calls me, 'George W.'—'George W.' I call
her, 'First Lady.' No, anyway—she said, we
said, march to war on our TV screen."

—Bay Shore, New York

Mar. 11,
2004

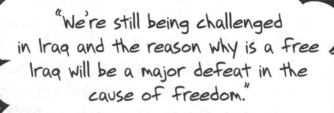

"We're still being challenged in Iraq and the reason why is a free Iraq will be a major defeat in the cause of freedom."

—Charlotte, North Carolina

Apr. 5, 2004

"They could still be hidden, like the fifty tons of mustard gas in a turkey farm."

—Washington, D.C., about weapons of mass destruction in Iraq

"This has been tough weeks in that country."

—Washington, D.C.

Apr. 13,
2004

"My job is to, like, think beyond the immediate."

—Washington, D.C.

Apr. 21,
2004

"I want to thank my friend, Senator Bill Frist, for joining us today. You're doing a heck of a job. You cut your teeth here, right? That's where you started practicing? That's good.
He married a Texas girl, I want you to know. Karyn is with us. A West Texas girl, just like me."

—Nashville, Tennessee

May 27, 2004

"Today I'm going to give you some reasons for you to put me back in office, but perhaps the most important reason of all is so that Laura will be the First Lady for four more years."

—Miami, Florida

Aug. 4, 2004

"Our enemies are innovative and resourceful, and so are we. They never stop thinking about new ways to harm our country and our people, and neither do we."

—Washington, D.C.

Aug. 5,
2004

"That's why I cut the taxes on everybody. I didn't cut them. The Congress cut them. I asked them to cut them."

—Unity Journalists of Color Convention, Washington, D.C.

Aug. 6, 2004

> "As you know, we don't have relationships with Iran. I mean, that's—ever since the late '70s, we have no contacts with them, and we've totally sanctioned them.
> In other words, there's no sanctions—you can't—we're out of sanctions."
>
> —Annandale, Virginia

Aug. 9,
2004

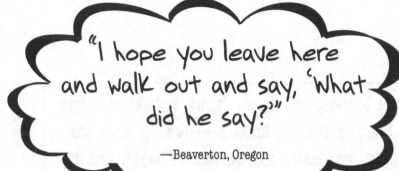

"I hope you leave here and walk out and say, 'What did he say?'"

—Beaverton, Oregon

Aug. 13, 2004

"Too many good docs are getting out of the business. Too many OB-GYNs aren't able to practice their love with women all across the country."

—Poplar Bluff, Missouri, campaign stop

Sept. 6, 2004

"Free societies are
hopeful societies. And free societies
will be allies against these hateful few
who have no conscience, who kill
at the whim of a hat-at the
drop of a hat."

—Washington, D.C.

Sept. 17,
2004

> "I think it's very important for the American president to mean what he says. That's why I understand that the enemy could misread what I say. That's why I try to be as clearly as I can."
>
> —Washington, D.C.

Sept. 23, 2004

"The enemy understands
a free Iraq will be a major defeat
in their ideology of hatred.
That's why they're fighting
so vociferously."

—Coral Gables, Florida

Sept. 30,
2004

"I hear there's rumors on the Internets that we're going to have a draft."

—St. Louis, Missouri, during the second presidential debate

Oct. 8, 2004

"Another example would be the Dred Scott case, which is where judges, years ago, said that the Constitution allowed slavery because of personal property rights. That's a personal opinion. That's not what the Constitution says. The Constitution of the United States says we're all— you know, it doesn't say that. It doesn't speak to the equality of America."

—St. Louis, Missouri, during the second presidential debate

Oct. 8,
2004

> **"After standing on the stage, after the debates, I made it very plain, we will not have an all-volunteer army. And yet, this week—we will have an all-volunteer army!"**
>
> —Daytona Beach, Florida

Oct. 16,
2004

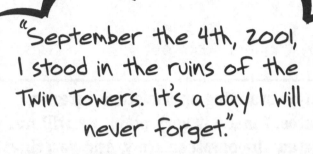

"September the 4th, 2001, I stood in the ruins of the Twin Towers. It's a day I will never forget."

—Marlton, New Jersey

Oct. 18, 2004

> "I always jest to the people, the oval office is the kind of place where people stand outside, they're getting ready to come in and tell me what for, and they walk in and get overwhelmed in the atmosphere, and they say, man, you're looking pretty."
>
> —Washington, D.C.

Nov. 4,
2004

> **"We need to apply 21st-century information technology to the health care field. We need to have our medical records put on the I.T."**
>
> —Collinsville, Illinois

Jan. 5,
2005

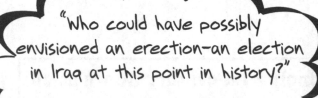

"Who could have possibly envisioned an erection—an election in Iraq at this point in history?"

—White House speech

Jan. 10, 2005

"Because he's hiding."

—aboard Air Force One, speaking about why Osama bin Laden is still at large

Jan. 14,
2005

"You work three jobs?...Uniquely American, isn't it? I mean, that is fantastic that you're doing that."

—to a divorced mother of three from Omaha, Nebraska
while speaking on his plans for Social Security

Feb. 4,
2005

"In this job you've got a lot on your plate on a regular basis; you don't have much time to sit around and wander, lonely, in the oval office, kind of asking different portraits, 'How do you think my standing will be?'"

—Washington, D.C.

Mar. 16,
2005

"[I'm] occasionally reading,
I want you to know, in
the second term."

—Washington, D.C.

Mar. 16,
2005

"I like the idea of people running for office. There's a positive effect when you run for office. Maybe some will run for office and say, vote for me, I look forward to blowing up America. I don't know, I don't know if that will be their platform or not. But it's—I don't think so. I think people who generally run for office say, vote for me, I'm looking forward to fixing your potholes, or making sure you got bread on the table."

—Washington, D.C., about the Middle East elections

Mar. 16,
2005

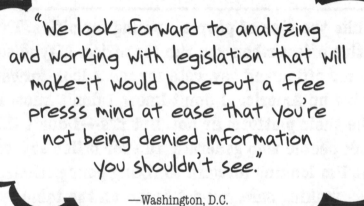

"We look forward to analyzing and working with legislation that will make-it would hope-put a free press's mind at ease that you're not being denied information you shouldn't see."

—Washington, D.C.

Apr. 14, 2005

"Part of the facts is understanding that we have a problem, and part of the facts is what you're going to do about it."

—Kirtland, Ohio

Apr. 15, 2005

"It's in our country's interests to find those who would do harm to us and get them out of harm's way."

—Washington, D.C.

"Well, we've made the decision to defeat the terrorists abroad so we don't have to face them here at home. And when you engage the terrorists abroad, it causes activity and action."

—Washington, D.C.

Apr. 28, 2005

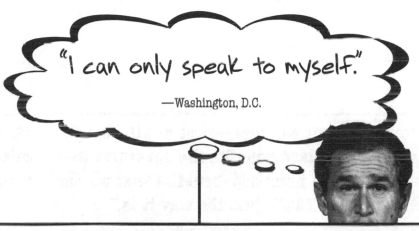

"I can only speak to myself."

—Washington, D.C.

"We expect the states to show us whether or not we're achieving simple objectives—like literacy, literacy in math, the ability to read and write."

—Washington, D.C.

Apr. 28,
2005

"I think younger workers—first of all, younger workers have been promised benefits the government—promises that have been promised, benefits that we can't keep. That's just the way it is."

—Washington, D.C.

May 4,
2005

"We discussed the way forward in Iraq, discussed the importance of a democracy in the greater Middle East in order to leave behind a peaceful tomorrow."

—Tbilisi, Georgia

May 10,
2005

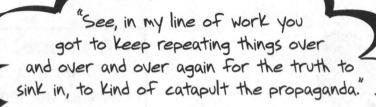

"See, in my line of work you got to keep repeating things over and over and over again for the truth to sink in, to kind of catapult the propaganda."

—Greece, New York

May 24, 2005

> # "We're spending money on clean coal technology. Do you realize we've got 250 million years of coal?"
>
> —Washington, D.C.

June 8,
2005

"Well, I appreciate that. First, the relations with Europe are important relations, and they've—because we do share values. And they're universal values—they're not American values or European values, you know they're universal values...and those values, you know being universal, ought to be applied everywhere."

—European Union press conference, Washington, D.C.

"I was going to say he's a piece of work, but that might not translate too well. Is that all right, if I call you a 'piece of work'?"

—to Jean-Claude Juncker, the Prime Minister of Luxembourg

June 20, 2005

"I'm looking forward to a good night's sleep on the soil of a friend."

—during an interview with the Danish Broadcasting System about his upcoming trip to Denmark

June 29, 2005

"The best place for the facts to be done is by somebody who's spending time investigating it."

—Washington, D.C.

July 18, 2005

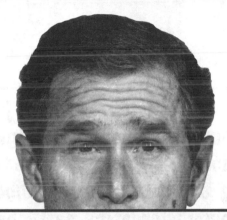

> **"My thoughts are, we're going to get somebody who knows what they're talking about when it comes to rebuilding cities."**
>
> —Biloxi, Mississippi

Sept. 2,
2005

> **"I can't wait to join you in the joy of welcoming neighbors back into neighborhoods, and small businesses up and running, and cutting those ribbons that somebody is creating new jobs."**
>
> —Poplarville, Mississippi

Sept. 5,
2005

"Listen, I want to thank the leaders of the—in the faith—faith-based and community-based community for being here."

—Washington, D.C.

Sept. 6, 2005

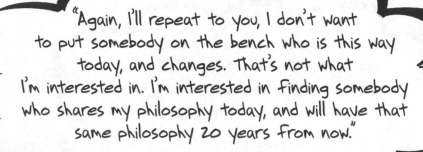

"Again, I'll repeat to you, I don't want to put somebody on the bench who is this way today, and changes. That's not what I'm interested in. I'm interested in finding somebody who shares my philosophy today, and will have that same philosophy 20 years from now."

—Washington, D.C.

Oct. 4, 2005

"I also remind them that I think it's important to bring somebody from outside the system, the judicial system, somebody that hasn't been on the bench and, therefore, there's not a lot of opinions for people to look at."

—Washington, D.C., justifying his nomination of
Harriet Miers as a Supreme Court Justice

Oct. 4,
2005

"Wow! Brazil is big!"

—upon seeing a map of Brazil at a meeting with Brazilian President, Luiz Inácio Lula da Silva

Nov. 6, 2005

> ## "As a matter of fact, I know relations between our governments is good."
>
> —Washington, D.C., speaking about relations between the U.S. and South Korea

Nov. 8,
2005

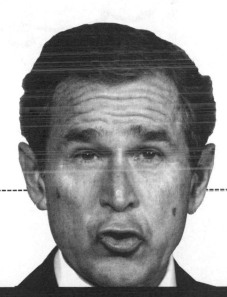

"We got the best workforce in America—in the world."

—Washington, D.C.

Dec. 2,
2005

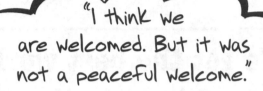

"I think we are welcomed. But it was not a peaceful welcome."

—Philadelphia, Pennsylvania

Dec. 12, 2005

"I mean, I read the newspaper. I mean,
I can tell you what the headlines are.
I must confess, if I think the story is, like,
not a fair appraisal, I'll move on. But I know
what the story's about."

—Philadelphia, Pennsylvania

Dec. 12,
2005

"As you can possibly see, I have an injury myself— not here at the hospital, but in combat with a cedar. I eventually won. The cedar gave me a little scratch. As a matter of fact, the Colonel asked if I needed first aid when she first saw me. I was able to avoid any major surgical operations here, but thanks for your compassion, Colonel."

—at the Amputee Care Center of Brooke Army Medical Center

Jan. 1,
2006

"You took an oath to defend our flag and our freedom, and you kept that oath underseas and under fire."

—Washington, D.C.

Jan. 10, 2006

"I'll be glad to talk about ranching, but I haven't seen the movie. I've heard about it. I hope you go— you know—I hope you go back to the ranch and the farm is what I'm about to say."

—Manhattan, Kansas, discussing the film *Brokeback Mountain*

Jan. 23,
2006

"He was a state sponsor of terror. In other words, the government had declared, you are a state sponsor of terror."

—Manhattan, Kansas

Jan. 23, 2006

"I like my buddies from West Texas. I liked
them when I was young, I liked them when I
was middle-age, I liked them before I was
president, and I like them during president,
and I like them after president."

—Nashville, Tennessee

Feb. 1,
2006

> "I think it's really important for this great state of baseball to reach out to people of all walks of life to make sure that the sport is inclusive. The best way to do it is to convince little kids how to—the beauty of playing baseball."
>
> —Washington, D.C.

Feb. 13,
2006

"No question the enemy has tried to spread sectarian violence. They use violence as a tool to do that."

—Washington, D.C.

Mar. 21, 2006

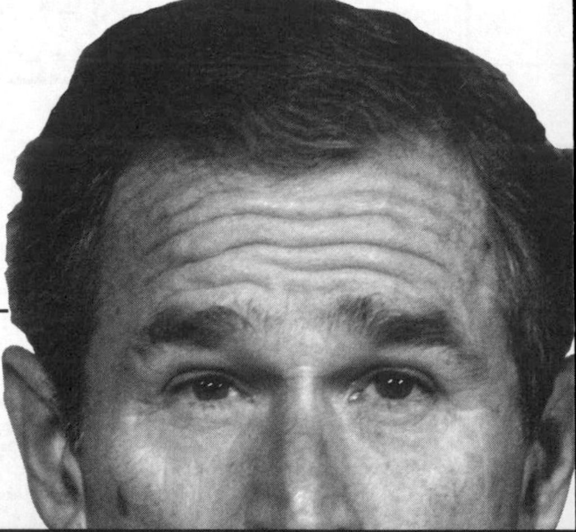

"I strongly believe we're doing the right thing. If I didn't believe it— I'm going to repeat what I said before— I'd pull the troops out, nor if I believed we could win, I would pull the troops out."

—Charlotte, North Carolina

Apr. 6, 2006

> # "I'm the decider, and I decide what is best.
>
> —Washington, D.C.

Apr. 18, 2006

> ## "I aim to be a competitive nation."

—San Jose, California

Apr. 21, 2006

"That's George Washington, the first president,
of course. The interesting thing about him is that
I read three—three or four books about him
last year. Isn't that interesting?"

—The Oval Office

May 5,
2006

"I would say the best moment of all was when I caught a 7.5 pound largemouth bass in my lake."

—in German newspaper *Bild am Sonntag*, about the best moment of his presidency

May 7, 2006

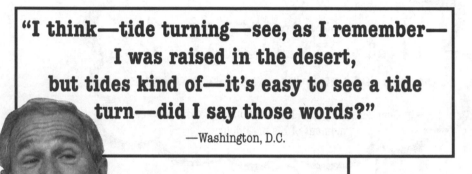

"I think—tide turning—see, as I remember—
I was raised in the desert,
but tides kind of—it's easy to see a tide
turn—did I say those words?"

—Washington, D.C.

June 14,
2006

Quote of the Day

Track your favorite quotes for the
remainder of Bush's term.

Quote of the Day
2006

Quote of the Day
2007

Quote of the Day
2007

Quote of the Day
2007

Quote of the Day
2008

Quote of the Day
2008

Quote of the Day

2009 and Beyond!